Four
Blue
Eggs

Four Blue Eggs

Poems by Amy Nawrocki

HOMEBOUND
PUBLICATIONS
Independent Publisher of Contemplative Titles
STONINGTON, CONNECTICUT

PUBLISHED BY HOMEBOUND PUBLICATIONS

For bulk ordering information or permissions write:
Homebound Publications, PO Box 1442
Pawcatuck, Connecticut 06379 United States of America
Visit us at: www.homeboundpublications.com
Visit the author at: www.amynawrocki.org

FIRST EDITION
ISBN: 978-1-938846-17-5 (pbk)

BOOK DESIGN
Front Cover Image: © Susan Montgomery (Shutterstock.com)
Cover and Interior Design: Leslie M. Browning

Library of Congress Cataloging-in-Publication Data

Nawrocki, Amy.
 [Poems. Selections]
 Four Blue Eggs / Amy Nawrocki. —First edition.
  pages cm
 ISBN 978-1-938846-17-5 (pbk.)
 I. Title.
 PS3614.A934A6 2014
 811'.6—dc23
                                                            2013044497

10 9 8 7 6 5 4 3 2 1

Homebound Publications holds a fervor for environmental conservation. Atop donating a percentage of our annual income to an ecological charity, we are ever-mindful of our "carbon footprint". Our books are printed on paper with chain of custody certification from the Forest Stewardship Council, Sustainable Forestry Initiative, and the Programme for the Endorsement of Forest Certification. This ensures that, in every step of the process, from the tree to the reader's hands, the paper our books are printed on has come from sustainably managed forests.

Also by Amy Nawrocki

POETRY CHAPBOOKS

Potato Eaters
Nomad's End
Lune de Miel

COAUTHORED WITH ERIC D. LEHMAN

A History of Connecticut Wine
A History of Connecticut Food
Literary Connecticut

Acknowledgements

Grateful acknowledgement is made to the editors of the following publications where these poems first appeared or were honored:

The Battered Suitcase: "Narcissus of the Finger Lakes"
Best Poems Encyclopedia: "The Nautical Why"
Blood Orange Review: "There Are People in the World"
The Chimaera: "Sensitive Skin"
Finishing Line Press: "Where Sky Begins," "Caesura," These Hours,"
             and "Ritual"
Flutter: "Gratitude"
Illuminations: "The World of Ideas" and "Achilles, Swift Runner"
JMWW: "Lucifer Falls, New York"
Lily Literary Review: "The Days of Claires and Jodies"
The Litchfield Review: "Annotating the Text"
Loch Raven Review: "The Beauty of Faces" and "Other Devils"
The Lucid Stone: "First U.S. Baby Conceived in Lab Now Seventeen"
Modern English Tanka: "Fiddleheads' Return"
The Newtowner: "Pickling" and "Still Life with Parsnips and Snow"
Phi Kappa Phi Forum: "Community College," "A Great Deal of
             Company," and "The Mail Drop"
The Shit Creek Review: "Postcard"
SNReview: "Threads"
Verdad Magazine: "Losing the Summer" and "Cleaning the House"
War, Literature and the Arts: "Broken Treaties"
The Wayfarer: "How to Say Goodbye" and "West Woods Cemetery"
Yes Poetry Journal: "The Thinker as Poet"

Contents

First U.S. Baby Conceived in Lab Now Seventeen

So what if she began life in a glass dish
or if the warm, red gelatin
which fostered those first hours
was not as good a vessel for life
as the real thing.
We all begin somewhere.

There in the lab's cold surroundings,
in a most endurable moment of quiet
the long syringe kisses the lip
of a perfect egg,
intimacy as precious and decent
as the real kiss,
shared between her mother and father
on their first date,
on their wedding day
on the moment they knew
kiss precipitates kiss.

For show and tell in third grade
she displayed the petri dish to her schoolmates
with the same tenderness and protection
she gives to the kiss she places
on the cheek of a boy on the playground.

1

In this her seventeenth year
on the bus ride home, she meets the same boy
as she prepares for ballet class and biology,
his hair the color of the polished brass bed
from her parents' bedroom.

Maybe she'll tell him on their third
or fourth date that she began
a tiny moment in a science experiment
in the square laboratory
blooming with beakers, vials, and microscopes.

Or maybe she'll save those kisses
until they lean tenderly into their fiftieth year
having shared enough moments of quiet
after the coffee cups and wine glasses
have outlived their color.

Sweeping Water Winding Past

Before the flood, the animals wept
small, undetected tears, like dew on the brow of a leaf,
curious about the coming of the noon hour
yet unable to fashion any courage. Left
beneath the fading gulp of sky, a swarm of bees
believing in destiny, watched the closing of dawn
and hovered, without fruit, in front of the ark. Time
only to gaze into the closing hub, turn and look
back for the companions left on the earth.

Once the Euphrates flooded, the Tigris,
with the sweeping water winding past
the unbelieving banks, rose away
from the earth leaving vital minerals
glistening like some far away spectacle of dawn.

Once this occurred, we were doomed,
settled out of the bargain with salt
in our veins, forever seeking the comfort of water,
from whence we originated. With our tiny legs,
and insufficient lungs, we slurped the air,
muzzled into a flesh that would betray us,
as would bones and extremities, as would
all parts of us that sought to be part of something else.
Knowing better, the soul, or what's left of it,

follows the path of the ancient rivers, around
the bend of time, struggling against currents left
and right of antiquity. Before the flood
our energies merged with one another, before
the torrent, our speculation had no boundaries;
now the source has run dry and earth creeps
into its prophesized ending. How soon
we forget how to bleed, and how to buzz.

The World of Ideas

The soul longs to return to the world of ideas,
Plato told us long ago, before the dark tomb of night
cloaked the Athens sky. This world, he thought,
holds the blueprint of every perceivable notion;
we tick beneath the shadow of that realm.

In an envelope of green leaves,
I recognize a crimson orchid, though
my soul perceives other versions:
a vanilla loam familiar to my tongue; the bouquet
brought into my nose by the mysterious story
of molecules which I do not see. To my touch,
the soft friction of petals butters my fingers.

Can I trust this as certain? If the milky blossom
reaches me in a photo, how do I know
this bloom? Somewhere the perfect orchid
exists and with it, a long tongued lizard,
a blue spruce, one stalk of pale yellow corn
with each kernel geometrically calculated.
This world of ideas houses the most proficient firefly,
my soul, and images the mind's insufficient
wiring can only dream of.

I've met this firefly before, my soul intuits.
I remember the wings, its resplendent glow,
pulse of instinct and repetition. I know
that orchids and glowworms met on ancient
Greek cobblestones, that Plato himself donned
a crimson sheath, bowing to the pleasant glow
of lightning bugs twinkling through history.
My mind does not play tricks, but frequents
these wonders when my own dark shadows
blink the answer to all questions.

The Thinker as Poet:
Aus der Erfahrung des Denkens

—Martin Heidegger

How like a whisper   the wind
engaging the cup of my ear.

How like a shout   these echoing
passages filter northwest to southeast.

How like a growl   the rustling leaves request
channel from shadows to true

existence.

How like a thought   disappearing
into thin air   these pages ruffling beneath
my pen   beneath a passing sun
        beneath the loud, enchanting

chimes of Sunday in spring.

Sensitive Skin

The universe has banished us;
fragile gauze hair on tiny forearms
succumbs to renegade heat waves
and celestial currents, which now and again
sabotage our bones, flaking and peeling skin
like pastry dough. Until we forgo
our ambulant nomad ways, return
to fur, or learn to play possum, our doom
will find us roasted and sagging.
                                            Perhaps
we should find our treeness, wear thick bark
and leaves that canopy over necks.
With years symmetrically bubbling
out of a center trunk, each milestone
would bear another ring of flesh
to shield the hemisphere's burley snarl.

Still Life with Parsnips and Snow

January leaves me
heartbroken as a snowflake
trailing from the cloudburst,
singular no more. Snow
has fallen in unshakeable rhythms,
fallen again and left itself
to swathe the unseen roots
beneath everything.

I stoke a practicing fire,
peel the parsnips' skin
down to the rooty white,
crunch the raw sweetness
before sending them
into boiling water, wait
in the reflective glow
of winter. Now iglooed
beneath an albescent world,
I blur with envy into
the vegetable underground
where starchy tendrils reach
for the warm hand of spring.

Lucifer Falls, New York

Like war planes, a crowd
of raptors scull through the blank
and cloudless sky. One
after another, they stream
over the open paddock
of midsummer green, advance
toward a still and speechless
line of trees. Their portents

reach the forest's door; needles
of pine brace between hard clay
and treachery. The bone black jaw
of a red-bellied snake ruins
a toad's last chance for escape.
He is in the middle of it now,
like the fawn whose femur lay
furloughed in the gorge,
trespassing on the slick ink
of river-smoothed black rocks.

Threads

Opening the walk-in closet filled
with the stuff of living—I think
one day we will have to sell the house.
In the meantime, closing the door
as a hatbox falls, there are no poems
about choosing the appropriate dress
for your mother to be cremated in.

As a schoolchild, I learned
when there is anything left over
you must carry it. I'm taught to love
what lingers—the timpani in a slow concerto,
the echo of a lost secret,
the sound three rooms away
of a breath stopping on its last chord.
Paying its debt, nighttime
closes its eyes and gives itself up
to morning. I think she is sleeping,
so best let her sleep. Keep the cat
from waking her.

I recognize my mother's hands
on the walls of our house. These are her threads;
the threads I hold onto as I make my way,
always there is a path back.

My first act as an orphan: I choose
the sapphire dress, the best color I know
depicting the moon's shadow
as it spirals away from the earth.

Annotating the Text

I tell my students to take up
their pens, savor the highlighter,
revel in the anticipation of appending
the words we make love to.
Most let their eyes follow the page
but not their untrained hearts, although
timidly, a few scribble whispers
on pages, becoming active, joining
in a dialogue with Bartleby.
One day they might revisit
these tactile memories, permanent
records of their comparative thought,
or maybe one of them
will remember this intimacy
upon finding, deep in the Tragedies,
her mother's small handwriting
on a copy of *Othello*, urging Desdemona
to stay the course. One of these daughters
will find buried in the basement
dog-eared, spine broken, her name
underlined with a star next to it.

Generous Bruises

At the bank, the teller catches me
counting on my fingers—the same feeling
I had chasing my sister's bike down
the unpaved road. She would fall before
I could catch her. As the road curved
I was thinking how little I have
to rely on; I should run faster.

Caught in the act of failing, used up again
dwelling in those Hopper paintings
where nothing vacillates, nothing
is weak, and all the women wear black pumps.
Their isolation—so original, it makes them
efficient, but keeps them separate.

But consider this: a crystal's structure
appears only when cracked. We experience
the same self when the *I* cracks
and our breath runs out. We earn
the favor of being by breaking
revealing a symmetry so generous it bleeds.

Watching a bruise heal from the inside out
it's the color that matters:
never black nor blue, but shades of yellow
and one hundred degrees of plum.

Caesura

After watching the logs crack and char,
heat stretching to my bare shins,
and daylight fading to its perforation,
the riverside tent closes us in
for a sleepless night. A nearby campsite
chatters into the late evening, and we beg
the shades for sleep that arrives only
with shackles. The July air is damp,
and I shiver beneath skimpy layers,
a mistake the cold night reminds me
to pay. With every sigh my waking self
catches the beginning of rest, only to throw
it back to the dampness. When the edge
of morning hacks in, we lumber up
and slug the short way to the foul
outhouse, then return to the dew-wrapped tent.
Grumpy, cold, I fold myself into you,
my head finding the slope of your chest.
Into the crux of sleep we fall together,
a shared pleasure we had never known.
We turn as one into the shell of a spoon,
your arms robed around me,
and in this posture, we fight the tremors
of the long night and doze,

saving bones from a frigid lair,
saving the next day from our sure
exhaustion. We flame into the now.

Antique Parlor

The old house struggles to summon
a story, elapsed from before it knew when.
Unplayed, the piano is dustless beneath

the portrait of two honest historians
who hang onto an embossed, flowered wall.
Beneath a splintered ruby vase,

a drop leaf table tunes out the ghosts
of the once-has-been and a nostalgia
burrows into the buttons of a high back

pink chair. When did these particular
artifacts settle into the orchestration
of matching dates etched on the underside

of felt? Once painted dancers fade from lamps,
wires coiled to electric plugs again realize
their uselessness and threads think fondly

about the loom and yearn to feel the soles
of hand-sewn leather shoes. Where is the glass blower?
Will the carpenter lament at the loss

of countable years? When will we feel homesick
for the marble quarry or lumber mill? Measured
in watermarks, the worth of a room depends

on how many future hands slip lace
over a frayed armrest or reach back
for an oiled rag before the clock needs rewinding.

The Yellow Bucket

Pulled from the rubble
of rusty chairs, ripped fish nets,
and deflated floats beneath
the beach house deck,
the yellow bucket, crusted with sand
offers its daisy-white handle
to my hand. Like a toddler
waddling into her first surf,
I put old toes into the silty dirt,
saltwater tickling ankles and rising
to meet my calves. Faded yet sturdy
the plastic bucket sits like a surveyor
on a flat rock looking over the breach.
I fill it with a few inches of water
and get to work.

Stepping lightly as footsteps cloud
the still water, I wait for clarity,
search for holes, survey the mud
for tiny announcements, and then dig.

The clam burrows deep
into the wet clay. I follow, bent
like a stork, arms shoulder-high
in the thick sludge, my face just above

shallow water. Before long
my palm cradles the scrappy quahog
and now the struggle is on. Against
the pull of its suctioning torso,
against the slow will of this ancient
organism, I extract the hard shell
from the dark muck of life, and carry it
from its water to the rocks. The yellow bucket,
itself a shell, waits for the visitor
who's snuck back into the safety of home.

By day's end the golden bucket
has been packed with clams and mussels,
filled with the silky darkness of sand,
and soaked in the brooding summer sun.
Gleeful, I carry the pail across the beach path,
slide the glass door to the kitchen
and prepare for chowder. Fingers
ache and black dirt has saturated
the ridges of skin and tunneled
under nails, proof of labor,
and testimony of both life and death.

Losing the Summer

Winter enters the body and it collapses,
the blood cells attack, the fever leaves
the brain with its patterns of coils
and discs like a red stovetop,
an alphabet of rivers and branches.
This landscape, contoured for activity, settles
into animal hibernation,
while remnants of ancient languages howl
from the hospital monitor.

Like dried sap on a tree,
crusted, yet viable, a small scar has left itself
after the coma—such a thing is not
a deformity, but a bud:
a seed replanting its succulence,
an isthmus back to the world.

Pickling

The pickle exists through the simple act
of preservation. Ever searching for the sea,
we mimic its salinity with a generous dousing
of sodium chloride dissolved in scalding water
and turn the whole thing over to vinegar,
to the chemical beauty of mingling molecules
agitating the turmoil of fermentation.
Whether the tucked leaves of a cabbage head
suck the masala pungency from the brine,
or thin moon slices of magenta beets bleed
from the sting of salt, whether mushroom caps,
round and fortunate, or carrots accosted
with the sweet spice of ginger root savor
the brackishness, everything springs
from the deeply plural earth. We store
the marinated concoction and thus safeguard
our futures, stave off our own rotting,
preserve all that is ancient and worthwhile
into one crisp bite of vegetable love.

A Great Deal of Company
—from *Walden*, by Henry David Thoreau

After the storm, the loneliness
does not evaporate. A half-day trek
to the shingled cottage through dunes
ripe with coyote tracks and unfriendly
dwarf pines means another week in isolation
with only the oily pigment of August
and the acrid stink of turpentine
to argue with. Even when the sun
in its naked, unforgiving callousness
ventures out again, holes in the atmosphere
remain. It could be worse.

A fourth trapped mouse rumors
to be still alive behind the shack,
and the ghosts of bums and poets ricochet
around the creaky loft. These, anyway, are voices,
consolation for the blank canvas in front of her.
A still life of bowled fruit decays in the charcoal
of her mind. First the brush must dip itself
into the clear water where the muses bathe,
but the well coughs up only the red iron of earth.

Once the mottled conglomerates
of sunset arrive, dinner is made; the wood stove

sparks against a damp log, the unswept floor
calls for a broom, and the burden of idleness
finally exhausts her. She dunks dry bristles
into wet, sandy paint, spreads black onto white
and forges a scene: stick figures walking
in the terrestrial moonscape of dune summer.
A blue crescent of water loops off
the feathered page, blurs past beach grass
to the deep, ample surf, its shores crowded
with the blinking eyes of sea gazers, each
with gravity 's sadness salted to one brush tip.

Where Sky Begins

Morning steps eastward over the island
but our window faces west, so we'll wait
until the day's luster swings around.
Over breakfast you tell stories about clouds,
the difference between the billowy meringue
of the cumulus and the bone-thinness
of the high cirrus vapor. I listen
as the atmosphere takes shape around us
and sunlight trickles down the table.
I muse at your smile, the polarity of your eyes.
After coffee, the ginger freshness of the island
entices us to cliffs and parading oceans.
But the scene is cloudless, as sky and sea melt
into their azure trickery, seamless and far-reaching.
I breathe into the surety that you are only
a step ahead of me, that the atmosphere extends
beyond us both, at least for one afternoon.
The permanence of blue will last a few more hours.
As the sun sets, we return to our linen room
and make love as white seraphs sprawl across the sky.

Losing Track

Before I can stop to investigate
or truly tend to this strange passage

of eerily bland molecules
across the blank, untended scope

of daylight, the baby ferns near the brook
have uncurled from their fiddlehead slumber

awakened into new greenness
and the towhee

has already moved on toward
the future blossoms of the laurel bush.

The Days of Claires and Jodies

On the refrigerator a note
reminds me it's time for a pap smear.
The months of Megs and Suzies
and the drive down Bronxville Road
in the green Saab for frozen yogurt
dissolve in the blue light of security phones,
as if life were a revolving door,
hiding the spaces behind the now.

Jenny knocks on our door with a box
of Swiss Miss under her arm,
the tea pot screaming, recalcitrant.
We ease into the surrendering
a third, sixth, hundredth time to a false security:
pullover sweaters, cold pizza, friendship
caged in the smallest dormitory on campus.
The oh-so-perfect night splinters
toward morning, returning to origins.
Then the semester ends
and the evidence of a world withers
and slithers like a garden snake.
The loss of friendship stings. Cowards,
gold diggers—these are just fancy names
for what we are.

The First Day of December

Three girls stay after writing class
to draft and tinker and revise,
discovering peculiarities
in an essay about immortality.
Pieces of advice tremble
on the edge of my sunlit lips
like leaves dangling from a limb
to be swept by winter's breeze.
Take a hint from history, ladies,
and do the right thing. Spare no substitute.
Open the spigot inside you and let flow
the fine glow of sugar burning like syrup.

But what have I to do with shaping
their lives—the way the wind
blows hair across a face?
We're not sisters or even friends,
and years separate us, connecting
only in the bindings of old books.

Community College

John's glasses hang by one arm, the bridge
of his nose dutifully balancing them.
Under the ubiquitous blue ball cap, gray
curls collect over keen ears, sharply greeting
the teaching of my voice, making sense of words
as they leave my mouth. Youth wrinkles
out from under the scrolls of his face.

I've never seen him without the blue
cap, and usually a paisley shirt, folded
then unfolded from a drawer down a street
somewhere. What does he bring in beneath
the graying eyebrows? When will the bridge
of his nose collapse like an origami bird
under the weight of his knowledge?
Balancing a book on his knee, the same knee
that balanced sons and grandsons,
he reads each page—each English word leaps
into his glance until class is dismissed.

He's my grandfather, fleeing Poland,
carrying a slice of babka in his satchel,
or an uncle, clutching a tug boat from Cuba,
making waves across the lonely ocean.
He could be one of the migrant workers

who picked cherries, tipped their hats, and whistled
as I swooned one summer in the heat. He
is a girl from Guyana, braids fastened tightly
to her scalp, dawn percolating on her face,
wanting to see the beginning justify the end.

In Direct Sunlight

A thousand gardens began in my father's mind,
in the spaces between the shade of maples,
in the basic outline of a perfect backyard,
in plots of patch-worked grass, in concrete urns.
There were days when deliberation
meant holly hedges, azaleas, iris bulbs
and rose bushes arranged with care, blooming
through many springs, giving life
to the house set back from the once-dirt road.
But mostly, what grew was what was left to grow,
weeds as welcome as pedigree.

Each year, white and green window boxes
housed pink impatiens and planters held
pansies and marigolds. Onions and chives, refugees
from the early years, returned again and again,
their trust of renewal something to admire.

He tried with seeds, never quite
getting the knack. Another garden began
in plastic plates saved from dinner leftovers.
Packaged kernels sprouted
in impoverished greenhouse domes;
the slight strings poking through black soil,
eagerly awaiting the future that never sprung.

These are failures of the small kind,
though everything is capable of resurrection—
another try, another year, more fertilizer.

He taught me this: having fallen
or broken, or been picked off,
a small branch could be rooted
in a water glass on the windowsill
until spiny white tendrils stretched out
in the cloudy glass ready to be planted.

On the day he died,
two glasses still lined the kitchen window.
The stubborn ivy had been there
for a long time unable to find its roots,
get its legs, helpless to let go
of the murky water. But once moved,
transplanted to a pot of earth,
the green returned—
a thousand and one gardens and counting.

Mechanics

Everything promised so well:
She holds the rock, smooth
about the size of a piece of soap
used to the tenth or twentieth wash.
Holding it like a turtle
as if it were alive
she pushes it from her hand because
this is how she handles anything,
and yet it dies over the water
on the hop as the arm snaps.
She is the turtle then,
age six wearing the pink pinafore.
Her sister has told her
she is really a boy
and she believes it.

As a boy she pees
on the rhododendrons, beats
the pants off other boys,
learns the mechanics of driving,
lug nuts and oil changes. She will jump
from the rooftop, pick scabs
and salamanders, eat them.
Funny, she even throws better.

As a girl,
this aggravates her,
this pulling of flesh on a hangnail.
She hides in the crowded closet.
Out of the starting block
it has already been decided:
she will learn to sew and negotiate
in a house divided.
On those ancient recordings
among the scratches and forced hiccups
of repeated skips, it seems
all the good storylines are taken.
First the head retracts, the legs, even
the tail. All escape to the inside.
This is the way it is.

The largeness of words
is heard on the stairway
after every storm. They seem
to repeat themselves. The boys knock
on her shell with their knuckles
but she is not coming out. She is not
coming out.

King Richard's Faire

Pine needles pen
a middle aged story—
the past laced tightly
through the eyes of a corset.
There are no true knights
but the vanquished,

and they lug beer mugs
on belt straps, tempt
puffy sleeved damsels
with sleuth smiles, yeasty mead,
and the suggestion of well placed
stag hunt scars. Everyone revels
in the metallurgy of make believe.

A joust rounds out the afternoon's play
while fire twirlers call off a threatening rain
and a boy with a plastic sword scurries away
like a salamander from a metal-studded
mother and stroller-caged toddler.

Spectators corral into the amphitheater
to gawk at the hybrid feline—neither
medieval nor malformed;

a whip-handed breeder advises
the charted steps of these muted stripes—
the forgery complete with a slurp
of milk, a put-on growl, the staging of height
and girth, so much tamer than expected.

Narcissus of the Finger Lakes

One might think excess—vineyard
after vineyard, lakes in multiple
with their glacial profiles, long, deep,
persistently appearing out the side window—
would prove too enticing; but like
the bulbous grape, everything awaits its finality.

Days like these make death seem easy,
like a butterfly's flight from one
round mouthed flower to another, no regret,
no disappointment, only bright August sun
and polished water. Even clouds
seem content, even a hawk, or the man
repairing the boat launch. It's all atmosphere,
all Riesling, Cayuga White, and Seval Blanc,
crisp and clean with notes of citrus
and green apple, a long finish that comes
with a few quick turns of a revolving planet.
So much sweetness, enough to sate old gods,
please lyre pluckers, and silence far-away echoes.

Other Devils

Once the bees ignite under my feet,
a brotherhood is sealed, a secret handshake,
a vendetta, the spiraling pinpricks
of worthy swords. Each sting—
an announcement.

Like affable torturers, they know
enough of pain to stop once the confession
has been achieved. What lasts
is not the sting, not
the swell of implanted knobs
from the end of lightning sparks,
not even the ache that spotted a few
honest branches of my body. No,

what lasts is the internal honey;
a shared fear: theirs—
entrapment, instinctual, ancient
and worthy of blooming now
and again. Mine—the dewy
awareness of having awakened
their sting by my stumblings,
the disregard for sacred land,
my foolishness for thinking hives

harbored only in trees, beneath
the overhangs of old houses,
in the compartments and symmetry
of the beekeeper's chambers.

And when the mêlée ends,
I am not killed; I am not frozen or left
bloody on the path. They retreat,
or else are banished by my struggle,
arms swinging, the flight of legs, a few
heart-shaped tears, a plea or two.

But I will carry their venom past the edge
of the forest. Soon the snow of a long winter
will encourage hibernation. Soon
I too will sleep, venom soaked,
loving the beauty of their defense
the swiftness of the attack and the humbling
victory. In my failure I kneel:
blessed, honey-full, immune to other devils.

Gratitude

If we could have read the moon's face
through the falling snow
that night we drove into its absent shadow,
it would have told us that the cold
sometimes melts things, too.
The train station, under hazy yellow lights,
fills with travelers arriving for Christmas.
We drive home with our father,
a faint smile crooked in the low end of his mouth.
Because the road hides so much,
more than once, Dad mentions black ice
the way he'd repeat an argument
until we understood. But when the car
spins momentarily toward the guard rail,
he anchors us—and we are held
by his steadiness, which, for so many years,
we mistook for other things—
discipline, scolding, but mostly anger.
It's time now to take this lesson
and file it safely under *black ice*,
reluctant blessings, how our father,
silver haired and breathing slowly,
saves his children's lives yet again.

Four Blue Eggs

Mother robin sits impatiently
under the clothesline, inchworm
in beak, returns to her bundle only
when the large figure that looms
above the timber of a false tree
abandons curiosity, tiptoeing away in stillness.

Day by day this foreigner
monitors the progress of the four blue eggs,
sneaking peaks through thin slats of the deck,
the nest settled on a rafter, underneath.

Before the hatching, roundness obscures
the odd disaster of pre-birth, squished
into shells, formlessly foretelling little
of future wings. The understudy

anxiously goes about her gardening,
gathering dry, paralyzed insects from between
the loosened petals of marigolds
taking them with her through the sliding door.

In hours, it seems, their beaks
open in curious diamonds. Unfeathered
and sloppily pink, the four breathe in unison

awaiting the next meal. Their winged
mother reclaims them obediently.

Abandoning the fledglings is not easy—
Unattended by a camera's eye, unnoted
in a field guide or baby book,
they'll lose their dinosaur shape too quickly
and disappear into styled feathers

and worm hunts. Despite the surrogacy
she has lent them, the watcher knows
their first take off will go ahead without her
before goodbyes are settled, before
her own feathers are wide enough
for them to flourish under.

Time Travel

The summer after the diagnosis
we visited their beach house on the Cape,
taking the route through those warped
highways, drawbridges, and rotaries
made for delirium.

What to talk about with my mother's friends
but the growth of children and the palace
of sea breeze, while the bug zapper
murdered hordes of bugs. What to say
of radiation treatment? What to say
of closure, that our meeting here
is the beginning of goodbye.

That night I met neighborhood kids,
joined them for bonfire and beers,
and dreamt of snakes.

Possessing What We Still Were
Unpossessed By

First, we see a cloudy blur of false revelations
that morning has unfolded for us. There is
a mountain high above us—we saw
its summit, so we thought, last night
as white throated sparrows sang in solitary
trills and rusted pines glistened in the dew
of the day's rain. Now we are hazed
into blindness and only fog can say
if there is a mountain or if there is not.

Even as moisture chills the skin
as much as wind, there's a teasing
notion that we'll make it from this wet
and saturated spot and walk into the sky
where ashen billows will break apart
and open to allow our passage.
Lichened rocks fill the mountain stairs;
diapensia and dwarf cinquefoil carpet
our steps as we plod through twisted pines
up the open face of the mountain. Cairns
barely visible in their stone camouflage
point with pyramid hands to the heavens.

Scurrying into the cover, a rabbit knows
already that we've been defeated; the wind

picks up and the rains begins to tumble.
Caught now between the force of ascent
and gravity's drag of submission, knees bend
and feet, unaccustomed to forgiveness, find
their best placement on rocks. We withhold
momentarily our awe, put away the notion
of grandness overwhelming our plans.
For a moment, or series of moments,
we think we can climb beyond
ourselves, beyond rock and height,
beyond ancient mysteries of evolution
and pressure to become part of the story.

But winds, with their haphazard motion,
are sure to tell us straight, without anger
or godliness: *you are nothing*. And whether
we call ourselves misfortunate or fool-
hardy for choosing this day, in our
unhumbleness we are lost. Bracing
against a rock, our minds debate
whether to continue. As long as we see
the mountain as a stack of forced steps,
we cannot retreat. But once we summon
without tears the words to say *go back*
we evaporate into the mist and surrender
to the slope. Then we finally find true
salvation in the land's certain wakefulness.

Ritual

Each night at dinner, in lieu of grace,
my mother lit the center candle
on the table. We children
were allowed two fingers of wine
from the icy jug that was kept cold
out on the front porch. The seven of us
shared bread and casserole on our full plates
and the light filled the room with luster.
Each of us had a task: clear the dishes,
wipe the table, snuff out
the half-melted candle,
its smoky trail reaching to the ceiling
like fingers folding into prayer.

When the washer was full,
we'd stand by the sink, my mother and I,
her hands plunged into the soapy water,
mine holding a dish towel,
removing the dripping pans from the drainer,
and wiping the water away, to expose the shine.
We'd stand there in the evening hour
quietly perfecting every keepsake minute.

Later in life, I stand in class, by the desk
in front of students as we discuss short fiction,

plunging into emerging themes.
A daughter and mother in one story
bathe together in a tub infused
with herbs and barks;
the same characters travel to market
to gather bread, butter, and fish
to prepare together later.
The mother preserves the daughter's childhood
in a trunk: plaid dresses and yellowed blankets,
mementos aired out and refolded again.

In capital letters, I write *ritual,*
chalk powdering the folds of my slacks. Together
we learn that these acts are connective tissue that bind
our muscle to bone. Though pages away,
miles, or even years, we, as characters
break bread, fold hands into each other's,
light the light that will unblind us.

Cleaning the House

The humidity this July afternoon
sucks the perspiration out of me
as soon as I pull up to the old house.
My brothers stand around the tall
green garbage can, sipping beer
and sorting the remnants of our father's
tool collection. On the garage walls,
rakes, shovels, and step ladders hang
like the museum items they have become:
a lifetime of utility, rusty and dented.
Wood chips and loose powder crowd
the table saw; an Adirondack chair
never finished collapses next to
drawers brimming with screwdrivers.

Good china packed in bubble wrap,
photo albums and quilts divided
among us, the antique sewing machine
carted away months ago with lazy chairs
and end tables, we sweep the house
of all our childhoods, mother's cancer,
dad's wounded heart. When our hands

have gathered enough, we smash
beer cans and hit them with a plastic bat

into the dumpster. Thunder breaks
through the thickness of the afternoon,
and we dance in the driveway, laughing
like the children we no longer are, letting
rain pour over what we cannot say out loud.

In My Sleeplessness, I Hear an Opera

In the beginning, I hear the darkness.
I am crowded by the soprano's knowledge
of body rhythms. I see I E flat cry.
And then the light bulbs begin to sprout, one
by one, by the side of the stage where all
the Presidents line up in order.
I know them by their thunderous tenors,
because when eyelids magnetize I do not
sleep. After that I pretend that I lay
in a coffin, my arms folded like white
linen in a closet oddly fitted
to the size of my body. I smell cedar.
But all this time I have been wondering
if my eyelashes have learned how to sing.

Present Progressive

the leaves
are blowing—

dead oaks and
paper wisps of
remnant birches.

beeches yellowed and
parched
brace against
the incoming gust then
abandon their stasis

as the wind
rustles elevated trees and
spirals into the
canyon of the driveway
donning a small
hopscotch of movement, the
leaves

are blowing. there is
no other way to say it.

the leaves are
blowing. leaves

blow; they move; they
flop and turn, tumble and
float; but not these—

these letters drafting
from high branches
with their testament
of weatheredness

are blowing. the wind
is gusting. I am

trying to be
present as these moments
are progressing to be
tricked, verbally speaking
into the inactive.

these trees
are watching; the cat
is following the
errant chipmunk who
is scurrying in a
frenzy between the

open mulch of last year's
woodchips and
the wood cover of the
porch stairs. they are playing

imaginary tag, the cat and
the chipmunk; the leaves
and the wind, and they
are active and

inactive like
the blacksmith who is sitting
and contemplating
the fire, the iron, the
movement before
it is time to strike as
the present

progresses into
the steely sum of
non-movement.

the earth is waiting for
its next hopscotch
moment; the cat is
moving her eyes with
darted precision. I am

staring into the
cortex of it all, the leaves
with their wandering lines and
pointed stems are
staring back.

On My Mother's Sixty-sixth Birthday

The hike is pleasant; the trail markers
are new, ferns and mountain laurel bloom
along the path. A soft whispering breeze
says something about remembrances
and a flimsy gasp escapes from my lungs.
Wishing for its own voice, a trickle of water
inches down a slope of jagged rocks as if
wanting just to touch something, however cool.
In a clearing, I see across the rounded tops of trees
into the valley and into the complex
gathering of green—the heart of June,
new and curious. Yet everything seems
to be empty. Despite the emeralds
all I spy are gaps; rifts appear where leaves
and bark separate, the gulf between earth
and sky is full of ever-present grey stones.
More than a half-life has passed
since we wondered whether the hair
she was losing would grow back black
or peppered with white ash, but I cannot
remember what we decided. Memory
in its detachment is as insufficient
as a summer waterfall.

Postcard

It's hard to dream, you write,
of a white Christmas on this bus ride
through the jungle of Central Africa.
It's hard not to think as I read these lines
that the beauty of this unpeopled landscape
of fog and trees holds some undeciphered code.
Paradise paired with sentence fragments
is how we communicate.

                                    We do not say,
the vice-director has accused me
of lying; Jamal's husband has committed suicide,
my house has burned to the ground.
These are for hiding in the folds of envelopes.

Instead we seek comfort, we say:
the glassy seascapes of Zanzibar
will take your breath away,
the budding minarets of Budapest
are something to behold. Look carefully,
your Italian lover should be somewhere
in this picture, waiting for you.
These words fill us:
A thousand houses extend
like bullet holes in the mountainside
over the sea.

Hannah, Who Feels No Pain

To suck her thumb like other girls
 is all Hannah wants; but she might bite
her fingers down to the knuckles, bloody
and knobbed. When paper cuts the tiny creases
of her small fingers, she feels no blaze of sting;
falling off the swing set, she can't detect
a sprained or ruined knee, blood running
and crusting. Kitchens, her mother warns her
are places of danger: hot coils of the stove
become as numb to her as the tart sun
on beach days, or sand filtering through toes.
The whisper of snowflakes and kissed pinpricks
of rain are shadows on a freckled face.

But maybe Hannah is lucky. Is she spared
from that twinge when her favorite goldfish dies
or what it means to fail at gymnastics and spelling?
Will she decode the bitterness of teasing
or understand heartbreak when her boyfriend says
I no longer love you? What if we were so lucky
to forgo toothaches and migraines, not to feel
our sore limbs at the end of a long work day,
or hear the scrape of our daughters' cries

that send us helpless to their beds. What if we
could have some of that luck, to never suffer
the salty wounds of sadness, become nerveless
and cold as lizards, biting our thick and bloodless tails.

First Mammogram

Around your waist,
the heavy
reminder of radiation's paradox:
destroy in order to save.

Contorted and squeezed
between those black
and icy plates,
breasts lose their pink.

On the monitor,
a white sphere glows
like a waxing moon
against

a starless sky;
bright, lunar plains
of tissue inherit
the elemental factions

of light and dark.
There are no blemishes yet,
no knotted anomalies
peering from behind

tungsten and detached electrons.
The silhouette
does not wane
but remains inert.

As you watch the screen,
this lace terrain of smoldering
luminosity is beautifully
static, killing time,

waiting for the variable
to appear, waiting
for the blackest night, waiting
for the new, undetectable moon.

The Nautical Why

By cowardice or courage
I came to walk the Cape
of Massachusetts
to rummage feet through dune grasses
and quarrel against tides, to tunnel
into the swift corridors of sea
and sand, and slip under the spell
of fragrant beach plums. To get

to the heart of it: the skeletal truth,
that unglimpsable mystery
which makes sailors leave
the thick yet shrinking land
and battle myths of octopus
and white whales. I want
to resolve the nautical why—
the question of density,
flotation and shipbuilding
inside and out.

I want to know, too, what makes
that great beast of waves and salt
spit back the pine hull
of an antediluvian vessel held
together with wooden pegs

pounded first by hands and later
hammered again by dense
saline fingers. After sleeping

for centuries perhaps, the shipwreck
lands in front of my own storm-tossed eyes
and I witness first hand what the sea takes
and what it gives back. Later

passing dunes, I see strewn among
quahogs and crabs, the ribs
of a seal, bone-white and eaten
with the same hull-empty shape
of the shipwreck, the same
twisted scroll that we all leave behind.
In the end we go to sea
for the taking, for the wreck
and its story, for the possibility
of opening the belly of the whale.

Naming the Flowers

Because the fire, tamed but fading,
makes us long for warmer days, we yield
to a spring urge to play and travel down
to the General Store still standing
since the days of zinc mining.
We are not botanists, you and I,
not rebels either, but betting
the sun will go down sooner
than we can return to the crock pot
simmering on the stove, we make time
and select names for the flowers peeping
out of the earth as the rain falls pepperly onto the grass.
Shining under our chins, we know the butter cups
because they are easy; their casual sweetness
makes me blush. Purple buds cover the ground—
delicate little mysteries—stretching across the fields
with the depth of the sea. After constellations
that sit high above the earth at night, we call
these blue-spotted knobs, Calliope. The small chalky ones,
Angela, after your grandmother, whose cheek bones
still sadden your smile. I say we should call
the falling rain drops Peggy's buds,
after the baby gone now a year,

who simmers and broods in my memory,
because a spoon sitting on the table
back at the cabin still reminds me of a round belly
now fallen concave.

Kitten's First Storm

She knows rain only from the inside;
sight first of a window pane latticed
with wet pearls, a few tiny waterfalls
trickling down, picking up bystanders
and new recruits—gravity's lesson
in obedience. At times, pitter-patter
plops past the rooftop overhang,
swishing down the house in the kind
of audible dribble that small feet
prancing on linoleum seem to recognize.
When the outside torrent comes
with windy fervency slapping against
a quiet house, she sleeps on the couch
unfazed by floods and unaware
that puddles well in misshapen circles
on the darkened pavement. When she wakes
she finds again the glass now streaked
with dewdrops, dripping, dripping toward
their rest. A paw tapping the sparkles
tries to catch their curious shapes,
touch the wetness of an outside world.

West Woods Cemetery

Sharing the ground with the low stones
of an old wall, a thickly scarred maple,
perhaps not even a sapling when names

were etched in granite, spreads its limbs
to shade a patch of club moss. In a hollow
high on the trunk, a family of raccoons

wakes in the midday sun. Tiny, patched heads
peek with sleepy eyes from the tear-shaped
opening; a cautious mother tries to shield

her suckling kits from those who might
steal them. A striped tail slipping through
the crease of wood or an outstretched leg

is reprimanded back into protection
of the den. Too small to venture down the tree,
the babies have not yet tested the dexterity

of their hands, never pressed an acorn
or frog between them, nor tunneled beneath
the fixed stakes of a fence. Chattering

like birds, they don't sense the luck of birth,
sequestered above grassy hummocks
half-empty with nearly forgotten tombs.

Soon they will learn the secrets of the mask,
how to face a moonless night and scavenge
the dull nocturne of suburbia. However crafty

and industrious the newborns become,
it will be hard to pass up the easy traverse
across a paved road, and scurry fast enough

to miss the black tumult of oncoming tires;
flies will swarm in silent thunder around
gnarled grey fur stuck in unburied rigor,
outstretched paws clawing at a thin gray sky.

X

Hector and Lillian carve their names
into the smooth beech giant, joining the other
knived insignias. Beech bark, unlike elms
or maples, doesn't shed; thus the carvings
will remain. It's good to know this
as a graffiti artist, but sad as a student
of Audubon. Hector and Lillian,
if only your love were quieter.

To mark our place is instinctual;
like dogs or bears, we need to leave stains,
cut into the earth's crust, destroy possessions
to prove existence. We even declare love
out loud, pissing on a nearby fence.
In order to invent a permanence,
we stencil bathroom stalls, shadow
a highway underpass with bubbled idiocy,
scar shoulders with ceremonial ink.

It's hard for Lillian and Hector
to realize that stars can etch
into the soul without leaving a mark,
the way you notch my heart with the knife
of your love, whittle an arrow
through the gray bark of my being.

Spinning Wheel

A slice of saffron in the autumn woods
becomes a thread the eye can follow
into next spring. It's the same with mothers,
their love is sewn into our character,
into the yarn of history, into all the befores
and the ever-afters we'll quilt ourselves.

We see her face when we look closely
into the structure of our smiles
or watch our own hands wash
and dry the dishes, plunging
our fingers into warm blue water.
Every time we look with love
at bluebirds waiting on the clothesline,
or see sunshine stenciled in a shadow
on the sidewalk; every time
we pull the quilt up around our chins,
we're colored by our mother's threads.

We see her standing behind the camera
turning the lens, snapping the photo
so our faces are clear and smiling;
we must only turn the camera to see
the earth stitching its path
around the sun, its filament
curved into the elliptical promise of return.

Broken Treaties

I wake to thunder, knowing that it is
in fact, thunder, not the grim catalog
of firebombs cruising through some other sky.
Turning over to face the clock-radio,
switching on routine weather updates—
the rain should continue into the day—
somewhere else the landscape breaks
with silver knives and august rumbles.

In the kitchen the lone shoot of a hyacinth
stands tall in a vase. I sprinkle
a dash of cinnamon into the coffee grounds
and read poetry in the nook
of the dining room; the clock
continues to push forward into
the open hours of our day, the storm
simmers and the rain wanes. I avoid
the news channel, don't enter the dimension
of those outside the white petals
of suburban bliss. I close my ears
to thunder, tune the dial to lowest end,
bury my head as the deejay sends me
further away from the weather of the world.
As the globe burns and shakes,
I plan for an afternoon nap.

Achilles, Swift Runner

It's the idleness that begs you
to be stationary when most of you screams
to move. A catalogue of gym classes
run through the mind on an old projector—
the last roll spinning to a clicked ending
as it speeds down—the final fat kid

remaining against a concrete wall,
standing still and shifting too much weight
from foot to foot, never running
to line up with the others: Sal Minolo
who called me Bozo at the bus stop; Beth Ryan
who snubbed me in the hall; Sam Smith
who wouldn't dance with me unless
the group filled into the circle around us.

The pummel horse waits with mats and onlookers
for me to crash my head against its folly,
and I want to run, swift Achilles,
to the far end of the horizon. Dawn
can mesmerize and keep me whole. So much fury
in the ankles means the great hills cannot claim me.

The day comes when stretching legs
on the family room carpet becomes

a trip to the mailbox, then, around the corner
and up the long slope past the fork in the road
where cool autumn breezes sing in eager ears
that survival means forgetting boys, kicking
the habitual ball of self-pity, punching
the horizon of possible pathways.

I am swift runner, born out of blessed dreams,
cool and uniform motion. As I go
I narrate my journey. I was the fat kid, look
at me now: Achilles burning
up the last hill. The victory is absolute.
I run another mile, just because I can.

Fin de Siécle

It's not as though the new highway
won't get you to the same places—
the Apothecary or Heritage Village,
locations trans-placed from other times—
but ambling past the Old Fire House,
the old road parallels
the Potatuck river that once powered
a lazy Connecticut town through the Depression.
On the way into town, the rubber factory
is now home to business offices,
and the print factory churns out
poster-board clones of Whistler and Hopper,
and the dust settles upon the stacks
like a snowfall. Ruth Watkins held on
with hands of steel until her ninety-second year
when Bennett's Bridge came down
and a traffic-friendly overpass
replaced the worn and toothless beams
and its rickety melody.

Once, from the highway,
you could still see, in the best days of fall,
pumpkins sitting like children watching a magic show
in the lot across from the post office.

It's been years since the shopping center went up
right there where we all believed
that the bright orange hue would remain forever
or at least into the next century.

Delta 88

He liked the American-made
roominess, the heft with which
the doors would sound their closing,
the familiar configurations
of engine and dashboard, and so
he traded red Cutlass Supreme sedan
for the cobalt Delta, two doors
for four, stretched his arm across
the front seat and drove the new Olds
until its sputtered and cranky end.

While other, more practical
family wagons with their untrunked
rear cargo space took over the garage,
the blue car lost its sturdiness
to winters, rain and rust. Even when
the muffler hung low, dragging
itself like an injured bird beneath
the rotting underside, coughing
with the insistence of one who just
does not believe the end is near,
Dad still drove the Olds fifty miles
down the Merritt Parkway to work
and back each day, spent weekends
in his shop coat replacing carburetors

and catalytic converters, hunting
in the molten landscapes of junk yards
for replacement grills and brake lights,
rebuilding when there was little left
to rebuild. Machines resign themselves
to such unelegant processes: combustion,
movement, friction, and decay.
They cannot go on forever, only
a few hundred miles more. Maybe

this is what he loved best: the car's
reluctant impermanence, the slow
decline to scrap metal debris, its long,
muffled refusals at the end. But mostly
that it was his two mechanical
human hands that kept it going
all those years and decided,
once and for all, to let it rest.

The Nest

A May storm knocks the hanging basket
from its rusty hook, the plastic cracking
as it falls. Tinting the concrete, the rain's imprint
outlines the fallen plant, fluttering fern leaves
spread out before my apartment door.
In my arms, I gather grocery bags
and walk up the stairs into the mess.
Thin green leaf-shoots spill
across the floor, and scattered dirt spits
out the tiny nest assembled with twigs
and cottony debris as three half open beaks
squawk tired pleas. I spoon the pink,
featherless kernels into their green home,
steady the rocking basket and slink quietly
inside. In the morning, I wake to silence;
my best imitation of motherhood a failure.

Arboriculture

I'm sure the red mulch
spread beneath the dormant azalea
has in its loamy peat the macerated remnants
of a massive Louisiana cypress.
I know it in my bones.

Somewhere in the swamps
of Atchafalaya, an ancient
colossus towering hundreds of feet
fell with the unheard echo
of a stolen temple bell. The harvested

trophy died again at the mill,
chomped to confetti by the grimacing
false teeth of a machine. I suffer
the russet sin with my arms elbow deep
in agriculture as I distribute

the ground cover around sweet william
and verbena blossoms in the front yard.
I'm hardly as wicked with those;
their plastic trays were purchased
from the farm stand where tiny, ripe

organic strawberries pleased my lips
and sour cherries melted like wine

lozenges in my mouth. I spit the pits
out the car window on the drive home.
But I am wicked to the core

and today, the supermarket is closer
to the mail drop and the library
where mediocre books, half-read
are overdue, and those bags of the dirty fill,
stacked on the concrete walkway near the store

seem so utilitarian, so earthy
and convenient, plus I hate the weeds
that the bag promises to squelch
and the neighbor, with her elegant
foxgloves and blooming geraniums is really
the one to blame for this. But I cannot

loose the swamp cypresses
from my mind, these conifers, these
sacred fellows holding the soil in
with their gracious roots, exhaling
with delicate silence. I feel like God

doling out the flood waters
with bloody hands handsomely disguised
by garden gloves. I am a fraud, a pirate,
and when the levees break again
I will sink into a counterfeit soil and drown.

These Hours

Because the daylight lasts
only as long as its breath will hold,

and the lapping Long Island Sound buries
its voice in the sand's soft pillow,
it is enough to sit and watch hours passing
like dust particles in a lighted window.

It is enough to face
this day's eagerness with a sigh,
to glance back from a shadow
to its origin slanted against the ground
and cover the lips' amazement with a smile.

Whether the light in these hours
of full bloom consoles or inspires,
it is enough to be next to trees, marked
like afterthoughts on a canvass
and straw-yellow grass peaking
through wet mud. That spring teases

winter with her sundress and winter blushes
these few hours in love,
this seduces me into loving
the seagull resting its feet in a tree,

loving it enough in the stillness
to reach without touching
the current and the waves. It is enough

to mistake this as accidental,
enough to swallow
the salt air, enough
for nighttime's glance
to be hours away.

The Mail Drop

Through the thin slit, the letter
collapses into gravity's harness, settling
face-down on the dusty wood floor
as the metal flap claps to its close.
The day's correspondences pile without
thought or purpose around each other:
a few catalogs, the weekly circular, a reminder
from the dentist. Not until evening comes
will anyone puzzle over the emptiness
of the left corner, or pass a hand
over the carelessly stamped postmark—
Judyville Indiana, June 14—cancellation lines
spilling over two stamps, not one,
together equaling the rate for an ounce,
plus one extra and unaccounted for cent.

It will be later still when a finger slips
into a tiny opening where moistened glue
failed to close, then slides across to break
the seal, reaches without anticipation into
the envelope, unfolds its accordianed contents
and reads: *I don't know how to do this*
except to say it plain: twenty-eight years ago
when I became pregnant, I thought the world

would end. It might be the last of the pile
to be picked up, no attention given
to its entrance into the house, slipped
without permission through a door's elliptic gap.

Book Club

In the months before he died
my father joined a half-dozen
mail-order book clubs. The hard backs
with their sturdy resolve arrived
week after week as his own pages
dissolved in vinegar. Even after,
the packages clogged the front step,
waiting for idle new eyeglasses, waiting
for a heart, bruised and bypassed,
to decipher conquests and romances,
to find that it was not unlike others,
full of the blood that would betray it.

I pull up to the long driveway
and find, rubber-banded to the post,
this month's arrival—the *Oxford
Companion to World Mythology.*
Instead of scribbling cancel
on the invoice, I crack the spine
in order to breathe the crisp pages in,
to decipher the stories that will have to fill
the spaces where my own heart failed.

There Are People in the World

There are people in the world, I'm sure of that,
seen with their comings and goings, umbrellas,
rain-coats decorated with black buttons
and the long belt that loses its way out of one loop,
nearly dragging on the ground. These people I know,
appearing in the long shot of a movie—exterior, train station, doors
opening and closing with magnetic pull. They're standing
clear, sidestepping the train's brutal electricity
and its indigo machinery.
                                    There are machines too,
I'm sure of that, inventions clean and useful—gears,
trapezoids, unfathomable windmills in far-away places
put there by men's curious hands, the systems
hatched from brains piquant and bloody. The train's careful maze
of nerve endings, synapses, breaks and rotors,
tendons of its apparatus.

In briefcases and tailored purses, the people
and their inventions mold this dingy world. They carry
metal philosophies, jagged pieces of technology—gadgets,
watches, cell phones, doodads to tinker and try out,
music and messages packed into files, accessible, tremulous.
The shoelace keeping the shoe in place, the shoe that eases
the foot down onto the heavy pavement.

Which do I prefer? The categories of people sandwiched
into their compartments, or their progress
that makes the train, the clock, the rails,
the beams and sinuous bricks bellow
in synchronicity—the track or the engineer,
the raincoat or the seamstress, the ticket, or conductor
punching my ticket, selling the fare, his face sandblasted,
chiseled, aching to tell me its ingenuity.

Cat People

After a while, the questions went away.
But even when the kittens came home
it was hard to convince my mother-in-law
that she had two new grandchildren—
the family we chose to be falls off
the flat map of expectations. Must we keep
our parenthood close or share it only
with the few who nurture and know?

I snuggle my daughter and contemplate
the mystery of her purr, smile with delight
when her brother crowds my knees.
But that is not enough. How to explain?
Perhaps this: the day my mother died
on the living room couch, we all slept
upstairs buried in blankets and scary
dreams, but the tabby bravely hugged
to her side, curled into an omega,
and kept watch as human night closed in.

The Beauty of Faces

We hold tightfisted to the beauty of faces
because photographs have no sound
unless we tap into the orchestra behind them,
try to hear the family's voices piped
and whistling the day they were recorded
as we can only imagine how glaciers
moving in and out of the landscape
create sound spacious enough to crack
the horizon. So, too, the hiss and spit
of the northern lights must be dreamed
because our ears are inefficient
as old telegraph wires.

           So the house
on South Colony Street carries
children's laughter up the front stairway
sloping toward the kitchen
where Josephine's peeled oranges hum
like music from the Victorola
filling the heart with remembrance and history,
pulling toward a place called home.

How to Say Goodbye

The eighth month buzzes
through lichen days, dry
and hot; mud pools sweat
from the long-ago decadence
of rain and frogs plop like ice cubes
into this imagined summer drink.

Badges of mica shimmer
in the sun-bathing rocks
and the thirsty earth sends
missionaries—brown mosses
crunching underfoot; leaves
absorbing the prism, reflecting
the short, electromagnetic
waves we have come to call
green, and grasses turning
now, slightly away as if
to say, *enough,* spreading
chlorophyll cylinders
to catch a dreamed of
rain drop. Even crickets
sing with parched voices;
their constancy interrupted
by an intermittent hiccup;

small bow legs pause to rest
and then return to syncopation.

It's too hot for human flesh:
our scales have fallen off,
and our naked, unprotected cells
do not photosynthesize.
We are much like sticks
fallen from hardy oaks,
vulnerable to the breakage
of heat. But there are promises, too
here in this parched world:
of shelter, protection, the sip
of a cool night, the awe of witnessing
something of change; promises
of relief if only we hang on until
our reddest moment, after we've turned
everything to sugar and can then let go
knowing winter's white can hold us.

The Fiddleheads' Return

When the first dew
of spring warms the early worm
out of hibernation
a covenant is rendered.
Young ferns, yellow with greenness,

nudge out from the deep,
snow-melted soil, poking through
centuries of death.
They leave comfort for hazards
of exposure, the burdens

of life. The new hope
coils slowly around the nub
of itself, the stalk
moves with incremental
sadness toward a timepiece

skies away. Soon
music forms at the edge
of delicate spirals,
music steeped in translation:
what loam says to darkness

in the cold moon hour,
how sunbeams brew the sacred
molecule to freshen
a poorly lit universe,
how the head of a fiddle

emerges out of
the clean violin of time,
strings tuned to the key
of true green assurance,
of repetition, the promise

of night music,
and the return of morning's
trusted, distant chord.

The True Weight

We make a list of all our favorite moments—
best hikes, finest meals— skipping
over the hard parts—when boots filled
with muck and rain froze our hands
and spun through the plastic
of our water-proof coats, each cursed step
you suffered through pain without ever
surrendering to sighs. Cataloging
the singular bluebell doesn't really

tell the whole story. The tiny tear-shaped
flower pressed between "A Dream" and
"Ode to the Memory of Mrs. Oswald"
in the pages of Robert Burns
does not relate the true heft of that volume—
the pages, browned and frayed, turn easily
one at a time but bound together
they hold the true weight of the poet's words.

So too, yellow broom and wood sorrel
decorating the ascent through Glen Nevis
or the heather spilling lavender toward
the modest peak of Bien Inverveigh
can never be summarized
in one sprig of tiny rainbow blooms.

Saving Myself from a Burning Building

Things are stackable—weight
on a bar, old expectations, cards
of a cut deck, worn hardbacks on a shelf,
stairs slanting skyward, seriousness,
silver: sixty-five kilograms. Tinker toys
on the spokes of a twig, they pile on.
Stack this morning's argument, all
the hang ups and unopened letters; stack
forgetting to learn the odes, pack
the yard stick and a warming globe ripe
with grasshoppers. Pile the lost manuscript
along with birthmarks and the laws of physics;
assemble the branches of genealogy crammed
and choking at the roots; stack them
like firewood. Heap tires falling off cars,
immobility, broken glass, mice eating their young.
Add missing Nina Simone on piano
in Paris when the lights dimmed. Cram
never playing soccer and wearing tee-shirts
over bathing suits; load sugared blood
and cells with their sticky membranes
metastasizing in the night. Stuff brain fever
and squeeze this ventriloquism into articulate
cannons and let them fire. Stack all of it

onto a forty-five pound bar, continue stacking
until the turmoil on your back becomes
a scarf around your shoulders; bend
your knees and press up away from the center
away from the earth; put gravity away into a box
beneath your feet. Squat down again, count
to twelve, then infinity; carry off the girl
you were before the summer, before
the spark, before oxygen. Carry yourself,
hair in flames, out of the burning building.

HOMEBOUND
PUBLICATIONS

AT HOMEBOUND PUBLICATIONS WE RECOGNIZE THE IMPOR-
TANCE of going home to gather from the stores of old wis-
dom to help nourish our lives in this modern era. We choose
to lend voice to those individuals who endeavor to trans-
late the old truths into new context and keep alive through
the written word ways of life that are now endangered. Our
titles introduce insights concerning mankind's present in-
ternal, social and ecological dilemmas.

It is our intention at Homebound Publications to re-
vive contemplative storytelling. We publish full-length in-
trospective works of: non-fiction, essay collections, epic
verse, journals, travel writing, cookbooks, skill/trade books,
and finally novels. In our fiction titles our intention is to
introduce new perspectives that will directly aid mankind in
the trials we face at present.

It is our belief that the stories humanity lives by give
both context and perspective to our lives. Some older sto-
ries, while well-known to the generations, no longer reso-
nate with the heart of the modern man nor do they address
the present situation we face individually and as a global vil-
lage. Homebound chooses titles that balance a reverence for
the old sensibilities; while at the same time presenting new
perspectives by which to live.

CPSIA information can be obtained at www.ICGtesting.com
Printed in the USA
BVOW07s1243020115

381644BV00001B/113/P